APPLICATION SECURITY ESSENTIALS

Security Architecture Series for All Levels.

Tim Coakley

TABLE OF CONTENTS

PREFACE

Hello and welcome to the challenging area of cyber security and application security! This book is written to provide you with the essential information as a guide, providing valuable summarised experience and knowledge to help you navigate the complex journey of protecting applications, and data, in an increasingly interconnected world.

As software and application development continues to advance, the importance of application security cannot be overstated. Each day individuals, organisations, and even nation states face an ever-growing array of cyber threats, ranging from phishing attempts to sophisticated nation state-sponsored attacks. The need for skilled professionals who can safeguard our applications has never been greater. This book is designed to help take you in the right direction, to be equipped with more knowledge and greater understanding of application security!

In this book, we aim to cover the field of cyber security applying it to the applications and equip you with the fundamental concepts and principles necessary to defend against a wide range of cyber threats. Whether you're a student starting on a career in Application Security, or a professional seeking to enhance your skills, or simply an individual interested in understanding the essentials of application security, this book is written to meet your needs.

We first begin by looking at defining some of the common terms used. We then delve into the fundamental principles of application security, discussing topics such as environment security, through to secure configuration and testing. As we progress, we'll look at the various layers of defence, including supply chain security and user authentication to name a couple.

Throughout the book examples are provided, to help reinforce your understanding and enable you to apply the concepts in the real world. After reading this book you will have learned knowledge and skills necessary to proactively identify and mitigate cyber threats specific to application security.

It is important to note that both cyber security and application security are ever evolving fields, with new threats, processes and technologies constantly emerging and being developed. While this book provides a solid foundation, it is crucial to stay updated and continue learning as the landscape evolves. The learning never stops!

The hope is this book sparks your curiosity, ignites your passion for all things Application Security and cyber security, and serves as a valuable resource on your journey to becoming an even more proficient cyber security professional.

ACKNOWLEDGEMENT

This book would not have been possible without the knowledge and experience learned from colleagues over the years up to current time, within the cyber security industry. We all stand on the shoulders of giants to succeed, and this book is a testament to that fact.

INTRODUCTION

Are you new to application security or cyber security? Looking to break into a new specialism or are you an experienced professional looking to expand your knowledge? It is possible for all of us to learn and achieve anything and I want this book to help guide you wherever you are in your journey.

This book will cover application security from the viewpoint of a security architect. Application security is not new, however what is clear is demand is constantly growing as the wider industry witnesses' various compromises involving insecure applications. It is crucial within application security, protections and multi-layer defences are incorporated into application delivery to protect data, services and people while at the same time working within constrained budgets and fast-moving technologies. We'll cover some of the basics, what is security architect and application security, then delve straight into the essentials, the important information you need to know and get up to speed and how to understand application security, what it takes to implement security and much more. So please enjoy this book and I hope it gives you educational value.

The upcoming sections will introduce you to one of the most overlooked areas, Security Culture. Looking at the human, how they use an application for good or bad, and also look at the various people responsible for building applications. This first section looks at how to engage, persuade and influence the complete audience of an application. People always come first, and application security is no exception.

The environment and where an application are developed is key to application security and with that this book will look at various areas where security is important. This will include some of the risks you may have heard of prior, covering hardware, software, monitoring and automation.

We then will look at the heart of an application, the source code. You do not need to be a software developer to read this section or understand this book. Data is often the primary target for cyber criminals and hackers and source code is another type of data of value. A section of this book will provide key areas and methods to protect any type of data handled or processed by a software developer writing code to create an application.

Next, we will look at the configuration of everything, this is where the application will be created, live and be hosted. There are many ways to deploy an application and with that many areas to protect as the attack surface increases. We will look at areas including virtual machine hardening through to protecting containers and hardening the cloud environments too. We will also look at secrets management and how to protect secrets, secrets that may be required by the application to function correctly, or by the user to be able to operate the application through authentication processes. Then looking at how to continue to protect an application through vulnerability scanning and penetration testing.

Following on from the security configuration aspects, a section of this book is dedicated to API security. Ensuring the application programming interfaces both to and from it are protected from cyber security threats.

The final sections will look at the nice to have security, these are also important, once the essentials are completed and the application security process is matured.

DISCLAIMER

The information provided in this book does not, and is not intended to, constitute legal advice, instead, all information, content, and materials available in this book are for general informational purposes only. Information in this book may not contain the most up to date legal or other information. This book contains some links to other third-party websites, these links are only for the convenience of the reader and nothing more.

WHAT IS APPLICATION SECURITY

Before getting into the detail, the first question to ask, what is application security? It is the people, process and technology used to protect applications from threats and known vulnerabilities and reduce overall security risk. The protection starts from the initial design of the application before any code is written and continues until the released software is decommissioned and is no longer supported. The type of threats to protect against are data breaches where the application is compromised and data is stolen, unauthorised access and any other act deemed malicious, depending on the laws and regulations of a particular country.

The ideal aim of application security is to prevent or reduce the chances of threats and vulnerabilities from becoming reality and exploited in some way. To do this it means understanding all the risks and looking at ways to mitigate these risks in advance, and as early as reasonably possible.

Application security consists of many layers of protection often dictated and influenced by the available resources, such as people available to do the work and financial cost to implement changes in the application or security.

WHAT IS SECURITY ARCHITECTURE

Security architecture is a role that in general involves the design of an organisations overall security infrastructure, systems and solutions. The role includes creation and support of policies, standards, guidelines and other general security documentation.

A security architect will review designs, perform threat modelling and both define and review security requirements, ensuring they are secure and appropriate security controls are recommended.

There is also some responsibility to assess and selection technology for security use, based on security and business requirements.

There is an element of risk assessment, which it central to security, assessing all risks relating to processes, systems and integrations within an organisation. Providing ways to mitigate identified vulnerabilities and threats with appropriate security controls.

The role also includes collaboration with business units, asking what is needed and building the most appropriate security solution into their ways of working.

Architects work at strategic and tactical levels and advise where needed. Given the complexity of application security it is common for security architects to specialise in application security in addition to general duties. The role of a security architect is a unique one working in many security disciplines, therefore knowledge of the essentials is, essential!

SECURITY CULTURE

This section will look at culture, specifically security culture. Culture itself is a loosely interrelated group of behaviours, beliefs and values. These values are not only company level written on paper, but also the individual level derived from our own lived experiences that we both bring into an organisation but also learn from within the organisation.

The security culture refers to how security is perceived, adopted and implemented. It is perhaps the single most important area within cybersecurity, arguably more than risk management. In some situations the lack of human resource, awareness and expertise in this area can lead to low security culture, and no matter how much money is invested the overall security team fails to deliver results.

Organisations with low security culture may experience more serious security incidents because colleagues fail to report issues or behave more irresponsibly, putting an organisation at greater risk. Contrast this with an organisation with high security culture, where employees take individual responsibility and accountability for security and do not solely rely on a security team to solve all issues.

Examples of a low security culture can include employees not regularly wearing their name badges in the office or not reporting emails as suspicious. Examples of a high security culture can include employees proactively contacting security whenever an issue is suspected, or challenging employees not wearing name badges in the office.

Dynamics of human behaviour, complicated organisational structures and lack of expertise, not just within security, but in general, can make this a complicated area to understand. Technology is very much simpler to secure as it is, at the lowest sense, ones and zeros, binary machines. People on the other hand are at their core driven by unpredictable emotion that can lead to unexpected outcomes, irrespective of their job title and responsibilities.

DEVELOPING THE CULTURE

Culture is something learned through observation or as a set of often unwritten rules that are accepted with little challenge and it can be pervasive. One of the areas to start are values, especially common areas that are shared amongst people worldwide irrespective of local cultures and beliefs. The most common values can be the most easily adopted by an organisation. Common values are the easiest for colleagues to both understand, accept and less likely to reject and challenge. Some example values would be focused on but not limited to:

• Integrity, these are values associated with being honest and holding true to life principles.

• Working in a team, where the effectiveness of a group can be greater than the individual.

• Ethics, the moral guide we use to control our own behaviours.

• Quality, a measure of our excellence.

There would be very few scenarios where these values would not be accepted given the global acceptance. To challenge them would call your own values into question.

The vast majority of organisations are hierarchal in nature. With a top-down approach to management it is natural for employees to follow the decisions of leaders. The leaders provide a critical role in culture that should be emulated by all, leaders should adopt and also demonstrate company values as an example to others. Leaders setting and maintaining positive examples of values in the workplace, make adoption by employee emulation much more likely to accept and follow. Leading by example should be cascaded through all management chains for consistency and reach. Examples of leading by example could be to complete cyber security training early, and when complete provide positive constructive commentary on the content for others to see.

Communication is also very important, if leaders and all employees do not feel like they can freely ask questions, raise concerns or leave feedback this can stifle culture. Communication should be as open as practically possible, however there will be situations this cannot happen, such as business decisions and board meetings. An employee working in an environment not free to ask questions is less likely to take more difficult steps such as the previous example of challenging colleagues not wearing identity cards in the workplace. However for the majority of situations, information sharing and giving all employees the ability to engage with colleagues is important.

That brings the subject onto collaboration which supports and promotes one of those core values we relate to, teamwork. It is not only about individuals in their teams but also teams working with other teams and inter departmental collaboration and information sharing. There is always a risk of teams developing into silos, giving a false sense of productivity as the team completes work. However silo working misses so many opportunities to succeed in areas that are simply not possible for a single team to achieve. By promoting greater collaboration there is a greater sense of belonging with more opportunities to develop. It is also very inclusive, particularly in global organisations where it can be felt some teams receive more and better work based on geography alone. More collaboration encourages a more positive environment, such environments make adopting new initiatives from security team easier to accept and adopt.

There are always opportunities to recognise, reward and even promote employees who show proactive contribution to an organisation. Recognising efforts of colleagues increases and promotes a positive constructive working environment. Recognition for promoting a positive security culture can be as simple as having your recognition called out in front of all your peers, to gifts, and new opportunities. It highlights to everyone that leaders are aware, are watching and value the contribution of everyone in a way that is inclusive. If everyone is valued no matter what the background or belief or how a person expresses themselves, it promotes a non-judgemental culture of acceptance. This reduces fear, uncertainty and doubt and increases confidence to raise concerns, comments and feedback.

Finally, in recent times implementing work life balance has become more prevalent, particularly with the more recent pandemic. This has provided an opportunity for organisations to create a work life balance culture allowing employees to work around their own lifestyles. This has been a positive for employee well-being as an alternate way to promote a more positive culture, building a stronger relationship between the employee and organisation.

PERSONAL MINDSET

One other area to mention is our own mindset, as an employee working within an organisation. Mindset is the beliefs and perceptions of the world, where security culture is concerned our mindset is what influences us to be positive, negative, or indifferent to promoting security culture. Therefore it is important to develop the right mindset in order to promote the best possible culture outcome all round.

We want to aim for a growth mindset, that is, to be willing to develop, change and grow. First recognising where we are now, our current mindset, our attitudes, beliefs and perceptions. Surrounding yourself around positive growth minded people, challenging your own self-limiting beliefs and perceptions. Continually learning and developing outside of the workplace and work environment. Joining seminars, reading books, in person classes and online courses to challenge and take you out of your comfort areas to change the way you think, behave and perceive under certain circumstances.

This subject is far greater than this book can ever cover in any detail, security culture starts with the person. Our own sense of responsibility, self-regulation, accountability and values go a very long way to helping an organisation develop a better more robust security culture. It is also simply good for you as an individual.

TRAINING

Training and education which is very relevant when related to improving culture. Education broadens the mind, creates open-mindedness, helps to deal with a changing world, and adapt quicker to new technologies and ways of working. With continued training and education, you will become open and flexible to change, and be relevant to the current working environment.

With greater education comes more opportunities for career advancement. Your employability and job prospects will improve, with greater chance of promotions or salary raises. As you complete training you may encounter like-minded students, together who share common interests or motivations. This can lead onto new opportunities and directions in life.

At the end of a long journey there is always the sense of satisfaction. This is the same when you complete any goals. Self-satisfaction cannot be bought, it gives a greater sense of purpose, accomplishment, and general inner happiness. This is one of the most valuable mindsets, the ability to want to learn, be curious and seeking personal growth wherever it may be.

All of the above contributes to a more positive security culture within an organisation.

KNOW YOUR SECURITY (KYS)

In any organisation, employees will spend much of their day following and completing their own responsibilities. There is a risk employees and teams will lose sight of, or be completely unaware of other teams, in particular security. It is important as part of a maturing security culture programme to advertise security throughout the business. This can include using all the internal social media and communication tools within an organisation, to maintain a presence, and to also create the image security is approachable for advice, guidance and support, not only for when things go wrong.

There are opportunities to share specific contacts into security, particularly teams deemed to be more at risk from security threats, such as finance, legal and human resource. Engage with them directly, give them appropriate contacts for business-as-usual activities but also 'hotline' contacts for much faster, personal response. It is good for company culture for all teams to present a human facing, empathetic image and avoid faceless ticketing systems that while are good for measurement and tracking perform poorly to improve security culture.

DOCUMENTATION

Within an organisation there will be an expectation of governance and oversight, an essential aspect to any application is documentation. This section will cover the some of the documentation required.

DESIGNS

There are many variations of principles available to help people design and develop applications. Irrespective of which principles you use to create an application, there will always be a design stage. The only exception to creating a design are solo developers, teams of one, the detail of which is never shared beyond the individual. In all other situations a design is absolutely essential.

Without any evidence of a design phase, there would be no way to assess the security, there would be no reference point, no understanding of application purpose. In reality there will be many teams that will be under pressure to deliver a product at an agreed deadline. That team may bring their experience from previous projects and apply it without writing a design. The lack of documented design does not prevent an application from being created, but it does prevent a security review.

How to convince development teams to create a design? At a bare minimum request a design diagram, a diagram will highlight the most important areas to assess and ask further security-based questions. For example where will data be stored and how data flows through the individual components. Diagrams are not too difficult to complete, especially compared against written descriptions where information can be lost in the detail. Pictures are much more effective for the broadest audience to understand showing what an application is and the purpose. However the caveat with design diagrams is that they cannot convey all information required to support a security assessment. The design diagram approach is a trade-off, better to have a documented diagram than no documentation at all. Ideally a comprehensive design document is the ideal, which also includes the design diagram as a sub section.

What makes a good design? This is something that invokes passion and discussion amongst security architects. The simple answer is a design can be anything that conveys an idea to an audience. It is ok to create different designs for different audience, there are no perfect designs. The internet will reveal how many templates exist to achieve the same thing, ultimately it is the reader, the audience, that needs to understand what the design conveys. More comprehensive designs should include:

Purpose, at a very high level, what is the overall purpose for the application, this can be a short paragraph that the reader can quickly understand. Ideally it should include some detail how it aligns with business goals.

Requirements, which are essentially a list of things that are necessary for the overall solution to operate. An example requirement could be for application data to be stored in a database. Requirements should also include security requirements too, for example all data in the database must be encrypted to maintain confidentiality.

Design diagram, or architecture design, represents the overall architecture which includes the component and how they are connected. This information should give the reader an understanding of the technology to be used. Ideally both the technology and versions should be included.

Data model describes how the data will be stored, where it will be stored and how. This can include database schemas and other data stores. This information should give the reader an understanding of what data will be stored and processed by the application.

Integrations describes external interactions, external from the application. This can be integrations to any other application, solution or resource. The information here should give the reader an understanding of API and third-party data exchanges as examples.

Performance describes any performance criteria and how many resources will be needed at low and peak demands including both data and user demand. The information here should help the reader understand how the application will scale up and down based on demand including any anticipated limits.

Logging and monitoring, all modern applications should have logging implemented to at least record application errors and unexpected behaviours in the application. The detail of the logging and how it will work is required to ensure it is sufficient in production to help diagnose and resolve issues.

Documentation should be developed, the design should include where all the application documentation will reside, the format it will be available and audience. The documentation is an ongoing effort all the way through to production and should be consumable to different audience, including developers, end users and anyone else associated with the application. The complexity of the documentation will vary depending on the audience, from clear and concise for end users through to detailed and complex for developers and technical users.

Support and management, during the lifecycle of the released application how will updates and patches be managed. This documentation should include the overall maintenance of the application and how issues are resolved when in production.

Compliance and regulations, laws and regulations applicable to the application, particularly the data being processed is ever more important in a globalised world. This can include data privacy laws through to payment card data processing regulations to name a couple.

As you can see there are different elements to a design and if one of these elements is not documented or accounted for, it can cause security implications further along the development process. These security implications can even extend into the release phase when the application is in production.

DESIGN REVIEW

For a design review to take place, a design must exist, in the previous sub section some elements of a design were discussed. It is essential some form of design exists, the level of detail very much depends on the available resource to create and maintain, at an absolute minimum a design diagram only should exist. As with the design, the review itself is subject to available resources. If a development team is small or subject to tight deadlines, requesting a lengthy design review process may not be a suitable option.

Design reviews are a cyclical process, in that once a review is complete, any changes will need to be reviewed. Also the design itself may be continually changing, maybe the technology changes and is updated or the requirements and business goals are modified. Any substantial change should require a review of the design.

The design review in the context of this book is application security. Based upon the design, does the application align and match with the intended purpose, does this meet or exceed the business goals.

The requirements may be aligned with the application without taking into consideration the security. It is therefore recommended to include predefined security requirements that are specific to your organisation, for example encryption requirements for business data or approved authentication mechanisms. In addition there may be security requirements specific to the application but not necessarily all applications, an example of this could be addition of a web application firewall.

The design diagram or architecture design, should represent the overall architecture, taking note of any technology that may be old, out of date or not in line with the security standards of the organisation. If there is any ambiguity of the solution components, clarification will be needed. The architecture design is also a great place to highlight where potential security controls will be needed or installed to support the application.

An assessment of the data model from a security perspective is necessary to understand both the type and quantity of data. For example does the data contain personal data, financial data, credit card information or medical data. The type of data may dictate the security, for example public data will not require encryption whereas any sensitive or personal data will require encryption at all times. The quantity of data to be stored is also important, if it is discovered the intended application is to store large amounts of data indefinitely this could conflict with country specific laws and require a modification of the design. Where the application is to be geographically hosted is also of importance as country specific regulations and laws may affect how the solution handles and processes data.

All integrations including API should be assessed for security as these are potential gateways into an application. All integrations should be authenticated, all actions involving integrations should be authorised with appropriate auditing in place so that there is an audit trail of all activities. Third party managed integrations, the vendors themselves should be assessed for suitability to process data, before being integrated with the intended application and with the organisation.

Performance limits should be tested later in the development lifecycle. Based on the application and its intended purpose, appropriate security testing will be required to test specific security use cases. Example testing could include brute force testing of the application login and authentication mechanisms or simulated DoS attacks against specific API. This type of testing can provide a quantitative assessment of the robustness of an application.

Any logging should be assessed for completeness to fulfil security requirements specific to the organisational needs. If the importance of the application within the organisation is high enough this may justify more resource. Generally less resource is allocated to the logging in favour of business enabling application features. Consideration for the creation and retention of logs for a defined period should also be defined, log retention is often dictated by laws and regulation that can range from weeks to years of retention.

Documentation should be clear and concise and include all the security decisions and controls that are agreed and implemented. The documentation should include how the application aligns with the organisational security standards, as well as laws and regulations.

Compliance and regulations consideration are also of importance, the design should clearly state any applicable laws and regulations. For example an application within scope of payment card storage will need additional security controls as a minimum, for example log retention for at least one year and data to be encrypted.

The number of design reviews to perform will depend on the importance of the application, as well as the organisational culture. In most business settings there may be limited time, opportunity and appetite to perform a design review, restricting a review to only one time. Ideally a design review should occur as early as possible to catch security issues early, training colleagues in security can help to mitigate repeatable security issues. At a minimum there should be an early design review, a review prior to implementation, as well as a post implementation review.

THREAT MODELLING

Another cost-effective way to catch the unknowns is at the design stage, through threat modelling. Threat modelling is more of a thought exercise where people in a room or shared call think of scenarios based on their background and experience that could occur. The more people involved and the greater the imagination, it is possible to identify those 'what if' scenarios and build the security into the design! The Shostack Four Question Framework is an ideal place to begin the threat modelling process, by asking:

1. What are we working on?
2. What can go wrong?
3. What are we going to do about it?
4. Did we do a good job?

The threat modelling process can be used alongside the solution design to identify weaknesses in the design prior to any development activities.

SECURITY STANDARDS

The design should be reviewed against a set of agreed and published organisational security standards. This is required for consistency, without standards the assessment of a given application will vary significantly with each new assessment. Standards contribute to the overall information security management and maturity of an organisation. Example security standards include but are not limited to:

AAA Security Standard, the access, authentication and authorisation standard. This type of standard defines the access controls to information and applications based on principles of least privilege.

Data protection and privacy, a security standard for protecting sensitive information and as the reference for ensuring the correct and up to date data protection regulations are followed.

Network security standard, as the reference for securing the organisational network infrastructure, including examples of tiered network architecture and appropriate network segmentation.

Secure software development security standard, as a reference to building secure applications, following the secure software development lifecycle.

Third party risk management security standard, as a reference to the assessment and management of vendors and suppliers involved in the application development.

Cloud security standard as a security reference to using the organisations cloud infrastructure and applicable cloud services.

Compliance and security auditing security standard as a reference point for application development so that applicable laws and regulations are followed.

IAM SECURITY

In this section we'll look at identity access management within the realm of application security. IAM is perhaps one of the single most important areas to protect and secure, and this is true across many security disciplines for the same reason, it is often the primary gateway in. Overlooking and not protecting IAM will certainly result in unauthorised access of resources at a minimum to complete loss of data in the worst-case situation.

IAM is a combination of people, process and technology to govern access to resources within an organisation, there are three key areas to protect:

• Systems
• Applications
• Data

Unauthorised access to one, can result in unauthorised access to all others, especially in today's world where IT resources are more interconnected, global and dependent upon each other than ever before. Applications and their IAM controls are dependent upon the criticality of the application as a general rule should meet a minimum feature set consisting of:

• User Management, being able to create, update, read and delete users. To cater for new joiners, movers and leavers within an organisation.

• Role based access controls, features to assign users to roles and assign specific permissions to roles. To be able to provide granular permissions in a simplified manner to control access and to grant the least privileges possible on a per role basis.

• Multi-factor authentication, where additional factors separate from username and password are required, such as a token number on a trusted device like a mobile phone. If the password is compromised authentication will not be granted without having the second factor.

• Single Sign On, support for authentication of users one time per session, users can be authenticated to multiple solutions and resources without needing to re-enter credentials, reducing the risk of credential exposure and loss.

• Logging and Monitoring features to record user activities relating to authentication including but not limited to successful and failure logins, as well as resource access tracking. This can help support auditing and also retrospective investigative capabilities.

• Special consideration must also be given to privileged access, and these are unique ways to access an application. Privileged access usually provides administrator level access beyond that of a typical user where low level access to the application, data and configuration is provided. These accounts must be strictly controlled and maintained, and only given to limited trained personnel.

Finally all the processes mentioned in this section should be documented as part of the application. This documentation should be understood by all users, from standard users through to administrators with privileged access. The documentation is also extremely useful to support reviews, such as security reviews by cyber security professionals.

SECURITY CONFIGURATION & DEFENCE

In this section we will cover the secure configuration and defence of the environments where applications are developed through to release. Not every single configuration can be covered in this book as it would be thousands of pages long. However, given that security misconfigurations are both a primarily and one of the biggest sources of security risks, this is largest section of this book to highlight the importance.

INVENTORY OF HARDWARE AND SOFTWARE

Within the development environment overall, a comprehensive inventory of assets is required. In fact this is a prerequisite to any secure configuration, to ensure each and every asset is known as it is added, updated and removed. If you do not know what you have, how can you properly protect it. Within a small organisation a small number of assets may be manageable, however once a business expands or if working within an existing large enterprise, it will be guaranteed assets will be missed and lost due to the sheer quantity of assets. If an asset is unknown it is impossible to identify any risks associated with that asset.

Assets not in an inventory may also be subject to incomplete or inconsistent security configuration. Unrecorded assets could become the single largest risk within the application development process.

There are many tools to achieve an asset register, this can range from an excel spreadsheet through to a dedicated configuration management database, referred to as a CMBD. Asset management will require a dedicated resource otherwise the asset list will become old, out of date and ineffective when needed to support security.

The asset inventory will need to include hardware assets including the virtual machines, containers, servers and any other infrastructure. The hardware asset list also makes performing vulnerability management of hardware easier to perform as all assets will be known and can be scanned, for example all internet facing hardware. A list of hardware reduces the risk of unauthorised access to unmanaged devices.

The asset inventory will need to include a software asset inventory, including commercial, free and open-source software. As with the hardware asset inventory, this makes vulnerability management much easier as specific software can be tested in related groups gathered from the inventory. However software asset inventories are more difficult to maintain compared with hardware assets. First, software changes more frequently consisting of major, minor changes as well as patches and security updates.

There are also the supporting library files and the more difficult to detect and record plugins, addons and extensions needed by some software. In addition the updating of software can vary based on system, so it is not uncommon to have multiple versions of the same software within the application development process. On a single server, there could be thousands of software and supporting library files present, before including any software specific to application development.

Environments with no software inventory are much more likely to be susceptible to many security risks. These risks can include running unnecessary obsolete software, increasing the attack surface unnecessarily, increased chance of an attacker finding and exploiting vulnerable software. Compromised software within development environments are more likely going to lead to compromise of other interconnected systems within the same environment.

SECURE DEVELOPMENT PROCESSES

The overall development process is central to the application development. The primary security guide for teams to follow are the security policies, standards, security guidelines, documented configurations, as well as training and development. This is concerned with ensuring the ways developers work remain flexible to accommodate a broad range of developmental activities and can do so in a safe and secure manner.

The entire application development team will need to learn and understand how to apply security to the software development lifecycle. This requires a greater security awareness from the application development team including but not limited to:

- Creating Designs
- Threat modelling
- Secure coding
- Vulnerability management
- Penetration Testing
- Approved authentication, authorisation mechanisms
- Security Logging and Monitoring
- Documentation

This will also apply to anyone with access to any of the developer pipelines, so can also extend to include testers, project managers, managers. Every development team will choose their ways of working, however security needs to be performed consistently.

HARDENING VIRTUAL MACHINES

Virtual machines can be deployed throughout the application development pipeline to support different solutions from code repositories, automation servers, and general developer servers across testing, pre-production and production environments.

It is therefore important to secure and harden any virtual machine. First the host virtual machine software should be secured, with the virtualisation software patched, updated and routinely checked for known vulnerabilities on a routine basis.

Use consistent build practises for the virtual machines, either by creating gold images securely configured by your organisation or purchase pre-build images. The center for internet security build and release pre-build virtual machine images that have been hardened saving significant time to manage this critical step.

Install security software where applicable on to virtual machines for security detection or security vulnerability management purposes. These will help to detect the latest known threats, malware and ransomware attacks to name a few. The agents also help to coordinate and manage known vulnerabilities discovered in the operating system or installed software.

Keep the virtual machines up to date, this includes patching the operating system and installed software. There may be some exceptions to this, and priorities may vary but generally all virtual machines should be kept as up to date as possible, to minimise exploitation of vulnerable software. Automated patch management is essential as the number of virtual machines grow within the organisation.

As part of the hardening process, unnecessary software can be removed, pre-build hardened images may not have all services and software disabled to maintain functionality for the user. A review of software and services will need to be performed to further reduce the ability for an attacker to exploit a virtual machine.

Access to any virtual machine should be restricted to either an approved user or service account in the organisation. Guest accounts should be removed, and any type of administrator account should be discouraged where possible. Accounts will usually need a password, and a strong consistent company policy on password strength must be used otherwise this could lead to accounts with guessable passwords. It is common for simple passwords to be used to make system management easier to perform, however this behaviour increases the security risks

Encryption should be enabled where necessary, given the low cost and ease to implement disk encryption, this can be included as part of the virtual machine build. Encryption can help to protect the confidentiality of the storage devices regardless of the environment it is hosted from test through to production.

Host firewall are recommended to be setup, particularly for the production environments where both inbound and outbound network traffic can be restricted and where necessary activity monitored. The host firewall on a virtual machine permits only the needed connections by known services and reduces the risk of malicious network traffic to and from the virtual machine.

Routine backups and backup testing schedules should be performed on at least all production environments. Backups should include the operating system and all the data therein, and also the configuration data of the virtual machine. Keeping granular backups will allow full or specific recovery of data. Backups are a critical part of the hardening process as it can be the only defence from attacks, especially ransomware attacks where an entire storage can be encrypted with no possibility of recovery.

Logging should be enabled, and this can include the operating systems logs as well as also any specific application or solutions installed too. The logs are in addition to the any generated by the security software. Collectively logs are sent to be aggregated and normalised where they can be monitored from a central point by security analysts. There will be many logs to choose from, it is unlikely all logs can be processed and monitored, the limiting factor will be too much data to process combined with the expense to process. All logging and monitoring will require its own infrastructure to support detection of any potential security risk.

Finally a combination of vulnerability scanning and penetration testing is required. Vulnerability scanning checks software for known vulnerabilities and alerts on any vulnerabilities found. These vulnerabilities can then be mitigated through patching and updating of software. Vulnerability management is an ongoing activity, performed daily, much of the activity is automated. The challenge is ensuring patches and updates are performed quickly to ensure vulnerabilities are kept to an absolute minimum and mitigated as soon as they are discovered.

Penetration testing is a much more involved process and is absolutely necessary to give additional security assurance a system is hardened. Penetration testing includes looking for the vulnerabilities, but this extends to vulnerabilities that cannot be detected using automated vulnerability management software. It is not automated and requires a dedicated penetration tester to attempt to successfully exploit discovered vulnerabilities. Penetration testing is essential for critical systems and for validating newly created golden images that will be used throughout the organisation.

HARDENING CONTAINERS

Container hosted applications are a growing target of opportunity. They represent a growing environment for hosting applications, shifting away from dependency upon server teams to build and maintain the traditional server.

As a minimum consider the following base security recommendations, referred to as SPOIL, for containers, consisting of:

Scanning containers for vulnerabilities and bugs using software specific to containers.

Patching and updates keep containers as up to date as possible to help mitigate known vulnerabilities.

Official or verified base images to build containers from official websites.

Isolate containers by limiting inbound/outbound traffic to necessary resources only.

Least privilege of installed software and users, where the minimum privileges are only applied to perform specific tasks and no more

In more detail, a container begins with a base image, either built in the organisation or more generally downloaded from an internet resource to be used to build the container. Official or trusted images are essential as it is possible for attackers to compromise images, post them on the internet where victims can download. Using verified images minimises this particular security risk. These images when downloaded should be hosted within a trusted registry that your organisation owns and manages.

Containers contain software for the operating system and applications to function. This software requires regular updating and patching just like a regular server, out of date software can become vulnerable to attack. Updates and patches minimise the chance of known vulnerabilities from being exploited. This also extends to the applications and their dependencies. Container patching management should be taken as seriously as the more traditional patch management already implemented in organisation for corporate devices and virtual machines.

Security software cannot be installed and operate in the same way as with traditional servers and operating systems. Security scans across containers and images is still essential, an alternate method is to use dedicated container scanning software that will search for vulnerabilities, malicious software and security misconfigurations. These scanning processes can be performed at any time with minimal impact to operations, this can be the only detective control for security issues.

Review all the software on base images and container builds, look for redundant software, unnecessary libraries and packages that can be removed. Containers are lightweight by design. However over time complexity can increase as developers in an organisation update their software and releases, with this in mind redundant software can remain.

Containers should be isolated as practically possible, primarily to minimise the blast impact, should a container be compromised other infrastructure will remain unaffected. Typically containers are isolated at the network layer, there containers may only access specific subnet of resources, where traffic can only be routed to other resources where necessary. Policies can also be created and applied to achieve this, for example docker security policies.

All roles must be reviewed, anything that can access a container should have the permissions reviewed . Using role-based access is the preferred way, by applying roles to perform specific actions and no more. Excessive permissions to perform any action within a containerised environment can lead to unauthorised access to resources or accidental misuse.

Benchmark documents are also available to aid developers to secure their container infrastructure. This can include using pre-build hardened containers. It can also include following guidelines to secure default settings, functionality and services prior to production.

One of the more challenging areas is logging and monitoring for security purposes. Containers are lightweight yet collecting and forwarding logs can impose a burden on resources. Logging must be retained, aggregated, normalised for security monitoring purposes. However the monitoring use cases should be carefully chosen and implemented to give some monitoring capability while at the same time balanced to not degrade the performance of the infrastructure. The logging and monitoring should consider both resource management and security use cases. Security use cases alone can jeopardise the daily operational management of services if security takes too high a priority.

As with virtual machine and server management, containers should undergo penetration testing. Penetration testing provides additional security assurance a container and the application or data it is hosting is hardened. Penetration testing includes looking for the vulnerabilities, but this extends to vulnerabilities that cannot be detected using automated vulnerability management software. Penetration testing is essential for critical container-based systems hosted on production environments.

HARDENING THE CLOUD

Cloud service providers create a much larger attack surface if you decide to use to host your infrastructure, it is a risk that needs to be accepted. There are multiple cloud service providers, each with their own services, which are similar, but not the same as each other. In fact each cloud service provider will offer thousands of services many you may never get to see or use. With so much complexity it makes it impossible for any organisation to fully secure. Yet organisations use cloud for the ease of deployment and perceived cost benefits. Cloud is adopted to fulfil business needs first and foremost, not security needs.

Cloud is typically priority driven based on data, so the type of data you are working with often dictate the level of security investment you will get. In application security if a solution being built includes payment card processing, it may fall under Payment Card Industry Data Security Standard, referred to as PCI-DSS and therefore get more security investment. Recognise early the data an application will process to help get security investment early.

Data is central to protect, ensuring the confidentiality, integrity and availability of data in the cloud. Knowing what cloud services are available to protect your organisation is equally important. Do the security services offered actually work as intended? Are they too expensive to operate? What is the development roadmap for cloud security services?

One of the most important overlapping aspects of cloud and application management is the configuration. Security misconfigurations account for a large proportion of cloud compromises, it can be the equivalent of building a multimillion-dollar home and forgetting to build the front door. Any cloud service used within application security must be reviewed, all of the settings should be reviewed for their security implications. For example if there is a checkbox stating encrypt data in transit, research the option, understand what it is and does, it likely needs to be enabled.

By default cloud service providers do not secure your infrastructure, the cloud resources upwards are the responsibility of the customer. Cloud misconfiguration and management is an ongoing process. Once a resource is securely configured, there must be continuous monitoring as a resource's configuration can be changed by users and services at any time.

> "Cloud is one big offshore config file, it's not a data centre or a physical server."

Secure authentication is the front door to cloud and to the applications, data and their services. There are several key areas to focus on as the minimum, MFA, IAM, SSO and API.

Multi factor authentication, referred to as MFA, this requires all users to provide an additional factor. In addition to knowing your username and password they also need to have something, such as a token generated on their personal mobile phone. In order to compromise the account an attacker would need all three, making it much more difficult to compromise.

Identity access management, referred to as IAM, this requires a centralised solution to manage both human and automated identities, and for each access permissions. IAM is the gateway into the cloud, it is therefore the primary area to secure. Securely configuring IAM early and creating the appropriate roles with permissions in the business means any application deployed in the organisation will use a consistent set of

IAM controls. Not securing IAM early can lead to inconsistent roles and complicated permissions that are difficult to risk assess, leading to hidden vulnerabilities and strong potential for unauthorised access.

Single sign on, referred to as SSO, within an enterprise greatly improves the security and user experience of any application that supports it. With SSO, the user will only need to enter their password once which will last the length of the session. By minimising the need to re-enter credentials the risk of credential capture by third parties is greatly reduced, for example such as shoulder surfing. Single sign on also to some degree mitigate the need for built-in application features that save credentials. Applications will use their own methods to save credentials, while this is a useful feature, the methods to store securely can vary, be inconsistent and be insecure using weak encryption. In addition, single sign on improves the adoption of applications in an enterprise by making them easier to use.

There is a section in this book covering API in a little more detail. However part of cloud security hardening is securing the often hidden and overlooked API, essentially all API must be audited, known and authenticated. There may be some limited situations where API are not authenticated, such as a public service, but on the whole it is another gateway into the cloud and all users must be authenticated to use it. API is more common as it is now a primary method to integration applications to work together. This can be application to application integration or application to specific cloud services. Often the integration is over the public internet and an enterprise will have millions of API integrations, which is an unmanageable number for people to deal with.

All communications inbound, outbound and internally should be encrypted. Transmissions between users, applications and cloud services must be encrypted to protect the confidentiality of data. As with API, there is simply too much information for an organisation to quantify, and it is growing year on year. Ideally an organisation will want to classify data and based on that classification use the appropriate security controls.

Given that encryption is much easier to implement in the cloud, it is simpler to encrypt everything in transit regardless of the sensitivity of the data. The key recommendation is to use the most up to date ciphers and remove any ciphers that are deemed to be weak or breakable. The cyber security industry is quick to report on which encryption is weak or strong and cloud service providers are quick to implement a variety of options.

Certificate management is an important and often overlooked area of security, yet it is essential for use in authentication processes and encryption management. Firstly a certification management platform is needed, within an enterprise the number of certificates required will grow significantly.

A central management service will track all the certification management and ownerships details. More importantly certificates must be set to expire at certain periods of time, this timeframe is set by the organisation, for example yearly. Therefore certification management must be able to renew certificate as needed to avoid disruption, revoke certificates when no longer needed and protect the keys that are used to create certificates.

Certificates are not only essential for external internet facing websites but also internal resources too. Servers, virtual machines and containers should all use valid certificates throughout the development process regardless of the environment. This applies to testing through to the production environments.

All data and code storage repositories used in the application development lifecycle should be inventoried and the data within classified. How data is classified will determine how the data is labelled or tagged, tagging allows for identification and automation of data.

PIPELINE SECURITY

The security of the developer pipelines within the cloud also need to be maintained and kept secure, as these can become a hidden gateway for attackers into application environments, and particularly into the cloud infrastructure itself. A pipeline encompasses the entire development process from beginning to release. As part of this both the entire pipeline and each of the development stages must be secure. Any misconfiguration of the overall pipeline environment and any stage of development can result in security risks leading to compromise.

Developer pipelines offer a great opportunity to strengthen the application security as it consolidates processes. As the pipeline is broken into stages, these stages can act as gates where different security tests can be introduced. Pipelines also offer the ability to segregate software development projects so that only specific teams can access specific code, offering increased protection to intellectual property.

Applications deployed using a pipeline are more consistent, not using a pipeline can result in inconsistent release methods, which in themselves can introduce security vulnerabilities. A good example of this is packaged software that contain developer default settings containing sensitive information such as user credentials, which should be avoided at all costs. The overall pipeline should be monitored, and many pipeline platforms provide audit logging options that can be periodically reviewed for security threats.

Secure developer pipelines are the modern method to develop software and offers rapid security integrations. With pipelines an organisation can better manage applications, improve application security and protect data and intellectual property.

SECRETS MANAGEMENT

Secrets management in the context of application security is typically focused on developers, testers and administrators working within the application development chain. Secrets can include but are not limited to:

• Passwords
• Encryption Keys
• Database secrets
• API Keys

Secrets are typically not stored and retained in one location, some secrets may reside within a dedicated secure store, some may be retained within an application setting, some insecurely stored as plaintext. Overall it can be difficult to track and maintain the total number of secrets for a given development.

It is recommended to use a secrets management tool that is dedicated to secure storage of secrets, these tools provide features to securely store, access and rotate secrets. Role based access is essential, applying least privilege to each role so that only the necessary secrets are shared based on a role and no more than necessary.

Secrets management, given its sensitivity must be monitored on a continuous basis for any suspected incidents. In addition secrets must be audited regularly, in particular for orphaned secrets, expired secrets or roles with excessive privileges.

LOGGING & MONITORING

Security logging and monitoring for developers is an important control, to be able to detect and respond to security incidents. Without any detective controls the security incidents will go undetected and compromises unmitigated.

Logging should be enabled where available across the entire developer pipeline. This includes the version control software, developer environments, test and staging areas, and all authentication services. Security events related to logs include successful and unsuccessful login attempts, build operations, code modifications, pull requests to name a few.

Logs should be securely retained, and with limited access so that logs cannot be tampered with or destroyed. Ideally logs should be stored in a central location, however storing in multiple locations that are convenient to access and secure is an equally common approach. The more centralised the simpler it is to perform analysis of the data in the most time and cost-efficient way possible.

The purpose of security monitoring is to detect security related events or incidents, it is therefore recommended the security team monitor and manage the security logging. The process of monitoring and security detection is time intensive and should never take time and resource away from development teams. The logs, if suitable, should be transmitted to a security SIEM, specialist security software that can correlate and analyse events. Monitoring must be continuous, this does not mean a person must monitor 24 hours a day, instead comprehensive alerting should be setup to alert security when a security issue is identified.

The final important point is regulatory requirements, which involve enabling and retaining logs for a period of time to be compliant. For example in banking where logs must be retained for a period of time to support potential future security incidents. Regulatory concerns also apply to the log content too, ensuring logs are not storing any personal or sensitive data.

Security logging is a critical security control and without it the application development will become a blind spot in an organisation.

METRICS AND MEASURES

With security controls including logging and reporting in place throughout a development pipeline, it will be necessary to demonstrate the value of all the time and effort of security implemented. Developing comprehensive security reporting in an application development is one of the final steps in a mature secure development process. There are many areas to monitor and where to start depends upon the organisation. Here are some common areas security teams try to develop first:

• Design Reviews. The percentage of designs that have been reviewed as part of a security review.

• Threat Modelling. The percentage of designs and projects where a threat model has been completed.

• Vulnerability management. The time it takes from discovery to remediate a vulnerability. Recording the total number of vulnerabilities and their criticality. Recording the number of vulnerabilities per lines of code.

• Security Incidents. The time it takes from security incident discovery to resolve the incident. Recording the total number of security incidents and their priority.

• Software Bugs. Software bugs can be a precursor to vulnerabilities. The time it takes from discovery to fix the software bug. Recording the total number of bugs and their severity.

• Security Compliance. The total amount of non-compliance against specific regulatory or company policies. The time it takes from discovery of a non-compliance to resolution.

• Code Review. The percentage of code that is manually reviewed. The percentage of code that is reviewed automatically.

• Security Testing. The percentage of code covered by static application security testing. The percentage of code covered by dynamic application security testing.

• Developer Training. The percentage of developers that have completed security training.

Metrics are useful to helpful to provide insights and help to drive and highlight where improvements have been made and where improvements are needed. They are also an extremely valuable way to measure the effectiveness of security expenditure in terms of reducing security risks and improving software security.

INFRASTRUCTURE SCANNING

The technology infrastructure once built is not immune to security issues. Regular scanning of the infrastructure used to host applications is required to identify known vulnerabilities, and this also includes misconfigurations. Misconfigurations are prevalent in cloud environments where the infrastructure is built to host applications and services.

A continuous assessment of all configurations of infrastructure, which includes cloud services is recommended. It is recommended a reference is used and followed such as the center for internet security, referred to as CIS security benchmarks. Benchmark documents contain the recommended configurations of specific services that maintain functionality while maximising security benefits. Additional actions can include removing or disabling unused services to reduce the overall attack surface. Other example configuration recommendations can include changing default settings, for example credentials to more secure credentials that are difficult to guess and break.

Hosted applications typically require network connectivity, requiring network ports to be open or closed accordingly. However the configuration of ports can be misconfigured or become misconfigured over time. It is recommended continuous monitoring of ports to detect open ports particularly ports that transmit sensitive information. Unmanaged ports are a common attack vector where an attacker can gain unauthorised access to systems and services.

Infrastructure scanning is becoming a more important requirement particularly in fulfilling, compliance needs which is becoming more prevalent demand on security. It is recommended to use an infrastructure scanning tool against multiple industry standards, such as PCI-DSS and CIS. All scanning must be continuous particularly in large enterprise where the quantity and complexity is high.

Infrastructure scanning results contain vulnerability data and therefore should be incorporated into the vulnerability management plan for an organisation. This is required to help prioritise and remediate vulnerabilities in a timely manner.

VULNERABILITY SCANNING

Vulnerability scanning is a security process which uses automated vulnerability scanning tools to identify known vulnerabilities in computer systems and applications. As with infrastructure scanning, identifying vulnerabilities before they are exploited is one of the most important priorities. Reducing the number of vulnerabilities reduces the overall risk to an organisation.

There are different types of vulnerability scanning, web application scanning searches for specific web-based vulnerabilities. Host vulnerability scanning searches for operating system specific vulnerabilities. Database vulnerabilities searches for weaknesses in database services. Finally network scanning looks for weakness in routers, firewall and other network services.

All vulnerability scanning needs to be continuous because the environment in an organisation is always changing, evolving and new vulnerabilities are being discovered all the time. Each vulnerability needs to be prioritised in order of which to fix first, because the total number of vulnerabilities can exceed the staff available to fix, fixing the most important first, the most critical is prioritised first.

Vulnerability scanning results are usually collected and aggregated into a central source for assessment and reporting. It is usually the owner of the affected resource that is required to fix a vulnerability and a fix is required within a given period of time. The more critical the discovered vulnerability the shorter the time to fix.

Vulnerability scanning is a core security requirement extending beyond the application. Vulnerability management is essential and is a discipline in its own right.

PENETRATION TESTING

Penetration testing are simulated attacked against systems and services, including applications. It is not to be confused with vulnerability management. The purpose is to not only identify vulnerabilities but to also exploit those vulnerabilities, proving that the weaknesses are real and exploitable, eliminating the idea of false positives increasing the evidence risk exist within an organisation.

Penetration testing is performed in a controlled manner, and the testing strategy is pre-planned. This includes scope, agreeing what can be tested and cannot be tested prior to testing. Due to the potential destructive nature of penetration testing, specific environments are used to limit the chance of disruption to an organisation. For example, pre-production applications are often used that are built as close to the production build as possible in terms of configuration and host non-production data.

It is important any testing activities are conducted with written permission. From a legality perspective, testing without clear permission and scope can be considered as an illegal activity in some countries. The legality is irrespective of whether or not a person is employed directly or indirectly by the organisation, correctly written permission protects the tester.

Most applications of importance will need to undergo some form of penetration testing. This can be by using a combination of automated and manual testing tools to identify and exploit vulnerabilities. Penetration testing also differs from vulnerability management in terms of the reporting. Penetration testing reports are detailed specific documents outlining all the steps performed, vulnerabilities and exploits utilised. Vulnerabilities are documented in order of criticality, and it is important to fix all vulnerabilities discovered in an application as quickly as possible and in line with the owning organisation. It is too common for penetration testing report findings not to be followed and recommendations not performed which means risks persist in an organisation, this should be avoided.

Due to the detailed manner of testing, time and resources needed, testing cannot be performed too regularly. Typically a test will reoccur annually, sometimes this period of time is shorter if an application is very critical and updated regularly. Single, one-time testing is only recommended if an application is of low importance and not updated very often. There may be other drivers such as regulatory concerns that mandate regular testing, for example such as PCI-DSS for applications processing payment card data.

CODE SECURITY

In this section we will look at source code security and protecting this vital data to ensure the security and safety of applications under development.

IDE

The integrated development environment, referred to as an IDE, is an application that is used to develop code. The IDE is not a security tool however it can be used to write more secure code if used and configured correctly.

It is recommended to use version control, most IDE will integrate into version control software to maintain and track all code changes across development teams. This offers a degree of protection from threat of code loss or destruction, providing that role-based access control is correctly configured. Applying principles of least privilege to developers who access code repositories, if needed, and code can be reviewed at any time for security related concerns.

Software addons known as linters can also be integrated, depending upon the development language being used. Linters can be configured to protect agreed coding standards within an organisation to create consistent secure code that is easier to review. It can also help to enforce security for example by preventing comments in code going into production.

One of the code features of an IDE is the integrated debugging, this principally allows a developer to walk through code line by line and inspect the memory and control flow. This helps the developer to spot and identify software bugs and potential security issues early.

Security coding plugins are also recommended when using modern IDE, as theses can allow quick methods to add security into the development. Examples of these are code that should never be developed in house by an organisation, such as encryption methods and authentication methods. This also extends to libraries that are used in code to add security functionality to an application, these libraries are tested and used by developers around the world and are more resistant to vulnerabilities when compared with in-house developed code.

Use automated code completion and AI assistants, this is where code is automatically generated for the developer as the developer is typing. This additional feature greatly reduces the chance of coding errors, particularly code that can introduce vulnerabilities. It can also make the mental process of development easier so that the developer can focus on more important tasks including secure coding activities. Note it is not a replacement for a developer, auto generated code is not excluded from code review.

The IDE is an application itself it is therefore important to use software that is actively maintained by the vendor.

Keeping the software in addition to addons and extensions up to date, particularly security updates to reduce the chance of vulnerabilities and exploitation of the IDE.

SECRETS MANAGEMENT

Developers responsible for writing code should also be aware of their responsibilities of secrets management. One of the most common vulnerabilities are developers using hard coded secrets, which are passwords and other secret information written as code. These secrets persist as plain text which means anyone with access to the code can obtain those secrets. This can also extend to configuration files forming part of the development infrastructure and support scripts. Numerous security incidents have been caused by secrets retained in code and later published on the internet, available for anyone in the world to discover.

Integrated development environments will provide extensions for secure handling of secrets that remain encrypted and secure and can be referenced in code using environment variables. Secure secrets handling can also be utilised using popular source version control software. It is recommended secrets management tools are used at all times and developers should never store passwords as plain text.

Developers requiring credentials or secrets need to make sure all credentials are changed frequently, and this includes API keys. Code should not be designed on the premise secrets will never be rotated. Code must be designed to deal with secrets rotation at any frequency interval.

Finally when using secrets in code, make sure that transmitted secrets are done securely. This means ensuring the development infrastructure uses strong encryption in transit so that credentials cannot be intercepted.

CODE REVIEW (SAST & DAST)

Code review by developers who are closest to the code is critical, however, to supplement and enhance this review process, automated tooling is also highly recommended. Static application security testing, referred to as SAST, is another method to review the source code of an application to search for vulnerabilities. SAST compliments the developer by identifying vulnerabilities missed during development time.

The scope of SAST is the developer source code, including libraries and any dependencies, anywhere source code is available. As a type of automation, SAST looks for patterns that indicate vulnerabilities, particularly those aligned with the OWASP top ten. For example SQL injection vulnerabilities may be detected by SAST, in applications that require access to and query databases.

A SAST capability can be introduced into the development pipeline into an integrated development environment and can assess code as the developer writes code. This means if vulnerabilities are fixed at the time of discovery, the total number of vulnerabilities at the time of application release will be much fewer, making the application much more secure and cheaper to develop.

There is different type of SAST to support different development languages and developmental platforms, each SAST require different levels of configuration. The output of a SAST can vary significantly from summarised reports to detailed output. There is a balance needed for the amount of time to manage and use SAST vs the benefits of reducing vulnerabilities. Security processes must not consume too much time from developers.

Another type of related test is dynamic application security testing, referred to as DAST. DAST does not directly review the source code, however it reviews the running application, the compiled and built running application. DAST is worth mentioning as this can be used in conjunction with both the developer code reviews and SAST reviews, creating layered application security review. Where SAST only requires the source code, DAST only requires the application to be executed and be running to work. DAST looks for security vulnerabilities and weakness while running the application.

A DAST tool will simulate an attack against the running application to identify potential security vulnerabilities. DAST can simulate the user and user behaviour and will use predefined attacks, some attacks for example are aligned to the OWASP top ten and other security frameworks. DAST can be used to test the API and application parameters, by submitting simulated user looking input and to monitor for unexpected behaviour.

Given the runtime testing, DAST can help to identify vulnerabilities where SAST cannot. It is therefore recommended to use both type of testing together. The dynamic testing can also be integrated into an IDE.

It is recommended to use both SAST and DAST however if implementing both, consider the amount of generated output. Is the total combined security output of the tooling and the developers time to review worth the benefit of finding vulnerabilities. The benefit may be worth it if the application is high value to the organisation or customer and if there is direct assistance from the security team. In some situations, such as low value applications and small development teams, using both SAST and DAST may create overhead and impede the release date of software.

OPEN SOURCE & THIRD-PARTY CODE

Both open source and third-party code is prevalent throughout all applications. So prevalent in fact that any organisation would struggle to inventory all instances due to the how it is implemented, not only in organisation developed applications but also packaged in purchased commercial software. Within modern application development these are simply an essential component. The challenge however is that both open-source and third-party code can introduce security risks into an organisation. Overall management is required and how this is performed differs per organisation, subject to available time and resources.

Third-party code can become a silent security risk when bringing software into an organisation in an unmanaged way. It is recommended to begin with vendor security assessments, this looks at the overall security of a vendor. An assessment looks at how the vendor perform security, handle data, review past security incidents and includes a review of their security documentation. A vendor assessment gives a good overall view of security maturity. Low security maturity for example could raise concerns for the security of code and products being sold to the organisation.

The service level agreements, referred to as SLA, are critical for the ongoing support of any purchased software. In the event of support requests to the vendor agreed timescales to respond to requests is essential. This also includes support for any security concerns, software enhancements, raising bug issues and vulnerabilities. There is also a separate agreement required on how a vendor will respond to a security incident and how long it will take to notify an organisation if it is subject to a data breach. The contracts in place should cover areas including data protection, and how security incidents are handled.

As with all software, third party software should be kept up to date, particularly security updates that specifically fix known vulnerabilities. Education and security awareness about third party code and software use is essential. Education to cover the security risks to an organisation as well as responsibilities of employees when using third-party code.

Open-source code differs from third party, in that there is no vendor, no clear ownership. Open source can be the collaboration of a group of people, consisting of up to hundreds of collaborators. It is therefore recommended to perform security risk assessments of all open-source code before using in software of significance.

Software security dependency checking software is essential for periodically checking dependencies for known vulnerabilities. Dependency checking can be performed from source code repositories as well as specialised scanners that scan dependencies, comparing against online databases and provide security advisories.

Covered in previous sections are code reviews and vulnerability scanning. Code reviews offer the opportunity to identify and document those open-source libraries that will be used in an application. Being able to build an inventory earlier makes future security initiatives and supporting security incidents much easier to manage. The vulnerability scanning including static analysis security testing can also be used, not only to identify vulnerabilities, but to also create a searchable record of open-source libraries used in an application. Creating searchable records are very effective methods to improve security assurance in the software components and their security.

An often overlooked element of open-source software is the licensing and terms and conditions. There is a common assumption that open-source code is completely free. Typically when using any software there is a contract that a user agrees to. Within an organisation it is important all contracts are reviewed and understood. Some licenses can include restrictions how the code can be used including in some circumstances the countries the code is allowed to be used and distributed. If building a critical or commercial business application it is important to understand the security implications of licensing, including open-source code.

API SECURITY

In this section we will look at the security of advanced programming interfaces, referred to as API security. As a common interface into applications, it is vital the confidentiality, integrity and authenticity of data exchanged and stored between applications and solutions is maintained.

TRANSMISSION SECURITY

The API section of this book is a relatively brief section however API security is a very deep technical subject that cannot be fully covered, further reading is recommended.

Information exchange is the primary use case for implementing an API into an application. As sensitive information is transmitted it must be protected from unauthorised access, tampering and interception. All transmission should be encrypted, API should use transport layer security, referred to as TLS to provide a secure communication. It is vital communication between the server hosting the API service and clients using the API service remain secure. HTTPS must also be used when securely transmitting API information over the public internet.

When verifying who is connecting to an API, both the client and the server must verify their identity. An example of verification and implementing authentication are using API keys, keys that only authorised users or services possess, without the key, authentication is rejected. Secure authentication prevents unauthenticated access to API services. Once authenticated, all authentic users and services of an API must also have a level of authorisation. Authorisation provides the level of actions and data a user or service is allowed access. For example it is possible to authenticate to an API service, and only perform very limited authorised actions, such as a found in guest access or read only access. Whereas an admin type role may be authorised to perform read and write actions and access all data via the API. The authorisation is typically managed using role-based access controls.

An API will typically be built to handle and process thousands or millions of requests, this is no surprise as they are built as a service. However API should not be built to transmit without limits. Once an API is benchmarked and peak traffic is known, limits should be implemented. Limiting the rate of traffic is important to preserve the service for all, particularly if an API is consumed by many users.

Rate limiting has another security benefit, in the event of a security breach of an API service the amount of traffic can be limited, therefore limiting the theft of data. If rate limits are reached the administration teams responsible for the API will be quickly notified and be able to respond to the potential compromise of service.

A final consideration are detective controls, in the form of logging and monitoring. Monitoring daily API activities, actions and data requests over time can create a baseline of what is normal. Understanding normal in your organisation helps to identify the abnormal. Abnormal detections could help to detect and identify potential security related issues.

STORAGE SECURITY

As API exist to retrieve and submit information, it is important that any data served via the API or any related API services are protected. Encryption of all data at rest is required and given the relatively low cost to implement modern encryption, it is recommended all data is encrypted.

Services providing data to any API requests should be protected, as mentioned in previous chapters the use of role-based access is essential. Only specific roles can perform specific actions on the data, minimising the direct human interaction to data as much as possible.

Given the consumer demand for an API can be high, the requests for data need to come from reliable and scalable storage services. If an API is made available to a global user base and the data store is in a single location there may be issues with availability when demand is high. The data store technology must also be able to support the most up to date encryption options.

The quantity and length of time data is retained should also be taken into consideration. Retaining data indefinitely can potentially lead to breaches in regulations and laws, especially if storing personal data or sensitive data unnecessarily. Storing large quantities of data could expose data to increased risk, in the event of a data breach the larger the data affected the greater the impact on an organisation including greater fines and penalties. It is recommended to keep data stored to a minimum using appropriate data retention policies.

As with the API transmission, logging and monitoring is necessary, particularly for any data access, deletions and modifications of sensitive and personal data. Without logging and monitoring it would not be possible to identify unauthorised access attempts as well as any malicious data destruction.

API RISKS

There is an entire resource geared to API risks, as such only a few examples will be provided in this subsection. In the useful resources section there is a link with a summary of the OWASP Top Ten risks to API. The list is a prioritised consensus-based list of risks related to API security.

The top three risks are related to one subject Authorisation and Authentication. Even though it is a fundamental security requirement to be authenticated and authorised for nearly all technology related activities, this still features high, as it is something not done or done well enough within the technology industry.

• API1:2023 Broken Object Level Authorization
• API2:2023 Broken Authentication
• API3:2023 Broken Object Property Level Auth

The fourth is another risk which has already been covered, when building and managing an API rate throttling should be built into the design.

• API4:2023 Unrestricted Resource Consumption

These are only a few examples of the API risks, the most common, it is highly recommended to refer to the OWASP regularly, direct from the website as it can change with potentially new risks added, reprioritised and old removed.

NICE TO HAVES

Within an organisation there will be many constraints to make an application more secure. These limiting factors could be lack of resource, people and money or be time sensitive. In certain scenarios priority will dictate, where some other activity becomes more important over others. This brief section will cover items that are more likely to fit into the nice to haves and never be prioritised and completed. Yet these stand out as valuable additions to enhancing and improving overall application security.

CHAOS TESTING

Chao testing are processes and technology to deliberately create failure and unexpected issues within a system. The type of testing occurs not in testing environments, but within production. The purpose is to identify vulnerabilities and defects within a given system or sub-system. The testing strategy is borne from experience that testing in controlled test environments will not identify all defects. There is always a chance resilience of production systems will fail and chaos testing is one additional technique to identify defects before they cause a severe outage or issue.

Chaos testing will typically be implemented and executed across numerous sub-systems that form part of a much larger system and is suitable for large scale enterprise applications. Testing is as close to real world failures that have occurred in the past. Testing techniques can include but not limited to storage failure, CPU exhaustion, loss of network connectivity and service corruption.

This type of testing can be designed to be continuous yet monitored for any events way outside of the expected test results. The primary purpose is to test how the application recovers and continues to operate. Recovery mechanisms can include service restarts, resource creation and auto-scaling. Ongoing review of results can highlight areas of an overall system that needs improving, changes to configuration such as over provision of resources at failure or failure to recover within a given subsystem.

Given the complexity, people and resources to implement and maintain, these testing techniques are likely reserved for large distributed systems serving a large userbase.

SECURITY ANALYTICS

Security analytics are processes and technology that can be used to reduce the occurrence of vulnerabilities, as well as identify and mitigate threats in the application security development chain. It is a complex operation primarily because of all the tools and technology each with unique data sources available, but also the variation of ways of working with each project and developers choose.

Data is collected from the various sources, typically development tools, and there are no fixed set of data sources. The number of data will increase over time and rarely contract. The data will be stored in various formats determined by each vendor of each technology product.

The next step is to analyse the data sources, aggregate and normalise the data, this requires reviewing every data source, reviewing the fields in each data source and determine if a field is of value. A data field can be determined to be of value individually or only becomes of value when combined with other data sources. This is an iterative process, returning to the data sources to verify and reverify field value. This has to be performed with the understanding of knowing what you are looking for.

With the analysis performed the security detection use cases can be built, tested and validated. The use cases will vary based on organisation, for example unauthorised login attempts would be a common use case, unless there are no authentication mechanisms in the application.

There are also integrations to consider, what if for example a security use case is triggered and that is determined to be severe and of high importance to the organisation. It may be necessary to integrate the most severe detections direct to the incident response team to investigate.

Finally regular reporting is needed, creating flexible reporting to suit different audiences that explain and tell a story about the data. This is less concerned about detecting threats but more about showing trends. For example it may be useful to show the time between a vulnerability in code being detected to being fixed to measure performance and risk to an application.

Given the complexity, people and technology to implement and maintain a security analytics programme. Security analytics is likely reserved for mature enterprises and teams that have been consistently developing and releasing secure applications over a long period of time.

RISK MANAGEMENT

Risk management is usually performed by a dedicated team of risk analysts. The risk information is refined and provided to management to help prioritise and direct security investment and resources where it is needed the most. At a minimum a simple risk register should be maintained for an application development project to record discovered risks during the development lifecycle. This register can be made available to the risk management team as needed. Some of the items that can be included in the register include but are not limited to:

• Asset Inventory, the affected items where a risk is identified should be included, this could be a piece of code, software product or person to name a few. An inventory of assets for an application development project should already be available making documenting multiple occurrences of the same risk easier to complete.

• Threats that could exploit a vulnerability in a given asset should also be documented. As covered in a previous section, threat modelling is a great way to identify threats to an application as early as the design stage of application development, before any coding begins.

• Vulnerabilities where specific weaknesses in an application should be documented. Weaknesses can occur anywhere from the infrastructure, server builds, software installed, codebase and even the application development processes.

• Risk Analysis is a more subjective item to document and requires assessing the likelihood and impact of each specific risk. Including what would happen if a successful attack and exploitation was to occur. This item is subjective as it deals with probabilities, and this view may differ depending on the job role performing the analysis within the application development team.

• Risk Treatment may need to be reviewed by the risk analyst within the security team. Essentially it is a summary of how to deal with a specific risk, of which there are four main accepted methods. Avoid, stop performing the activities that are causing the risk in the first instance. Mitigation/reduction, methods to reduce the likelihood and impact of a given risk. Transfer the risk to another so that a third party can accept it. Finally, risk acceptance, which is to accept the risk as it is documented with the understanding the risk will remain.

As you can see a lot of information is needed for each entry within a risk register to be effective. Application security is complex, and the number of risks per project can be substantial. In addition development and project management teams are usually stretched to delivering the product to the business in time, usually under strict deadlines to maintain a competitive edge. This is why risk management, although critical and central to security falls into the nice to have category for those delivering products. However whenever possible risks should be documented and managed.

SUMMARY

This book covered many of the essential areas key to a security practitioner working in the field of application security. This book is part of the security architecture series aimed at designing security early into specialist technical areas, explaining the essentials.

Many of the topics in this book are subjects in their own right, as this book covers the areas you must focus on first. Each topic requires further research, working in a team, to develop and mature within your own organisation, specific to your own people, organisational processes and chosen technology.

We covered security culture and how this is fundamental across all security disciplines, it is the most important and often overlooked area. If you have good security culture, the organisation will be safer, if you have poor security culture, the organisation is put at greater risk unnecessarily. It is important to create and maintain a positive culture alongside all other work activities and it is something everyone is responsible for and for the leaders to be the role models.

Training was also covered, we all need to learn skills to develop and improve, training is a continuous lifetime process. Within cybersecurity, training is essential simply because new technology, new ideas, and security threats and landscape is constantly changing and evolving. Training is not only good for gaining knowledge, it is good for creating a positive growth mindset and contributes to a positive working culture with new ideas and ways of working.

Documentation was discussed, applications cannot be developed without documentation, and security documentation is now an essential. Everything starts with a design that is documented and shared to an audience who will understand the purpose before any work starts, it is also a good opportunity to identify security risks as early as possible. Threat modelling is an essential early step to help draw out security risks, simply by using a design and by working as a team. There is a clear financial benefit to being better prepared before commencing any expensive work. We also covered how security standards contribute to the overall information security management to help reduce organisational security risk.

IAM is a cornerstone of security, the primary gateway into the services and software and into an organisation, the single most important area to protect. We covered the different security requirements as a minimum to protect an application. Role based access was covered to provide granular permissions in the most efficient manner possible. Both multi-factor authentication and single sign on for authentication were discussed providing an exponential level of increased security when both used in an enterprise.

A large section of the essentials focused on secure configuration, as it is the misconfigurations in an environment that cause the biggest security risks, particularly when combined together. This starts with knowing what assets you have when building an application, building the inventory of hardware and software assets. The overall secure development process needs to be documented and documentation followed, including the configuration of all the tools in the pipeline. Hardware including virtual machines, containers and anything else hosting applications need to be hardened to better withstand security threats, this includes all components used within cloud environments, vastly expanding an organisations footprint.

We also looked at the pipeline, the start and end stages of application development, securing each stage in the pipeline to prevent compromise of the entire developer chain. Secrets and credentials used throughout the application development process is also important, if the environment is secure but the secrets are not, it can be an invitation to compromise. Secrets management extends beyond the user to service accounts and database access and encryption key protection.

A large part of a security programme are the detective controls, can an organisation detect security issues as they occur. A part of this book covered logging and monitoring, setting up the ability to find security issues throughout the application development process. Lastly as part of the secure configuration, vulnerability scanning and penetration testing was covered, which provides a combination of continuous vulnerability detection and periodic detailed penetration testing by exploiting and testing flaws in an application.

A section of this book covered the code and securing the code, starting with the IDE, the place where the developer creates the software and primary location to also introduce vulnerabilities. The IDE is an ideal place to introduce security early, using automation tools with security scanning capabilities. As part of code security, secrets management is covered again as secrets are inadvertently introduced into code by developers and testers which can create a serious risk to any application.

Expanding on the IDE, we covered both SAST and DAST, two separate methods that complement each other to identify security risks and vulnerabilities. We then looked at both third-party and open-source code, this is code written by other developers and brought into an organisation as trusted code, looking at methods to reduce the overall risk when using these essential resources in modern software development.

We then moved onto API security, a common gateway into an application for attackers to exploit. API is a technical topic, summarising the essential areas to protect when API are implemented. Covering transmission and data stored within the API infrastructure as well as where to find the top API risks to help you prioritise where to start securing your API.

Finally this book included some other areas that while not essential would be important to consider within the application security programme, including chaos testing, risk management and detailed security analytics.

It is important to remember security is a continuous journey of improvement rather than an end goal with everything completed. With that, thank you for taking a few steps with me in your journey with this book.

Oh, and if you can, please leave a rating for my book if it has helped you. Good luck and take care.

USEFUL RESOURCES

A small collection of resources for continued learning after reading this book. Enjoy!

RECOMMENDED BOOKS

Shostack, Adam. *Threat Modeling: Designing for Security*. John Wiley & Sons, 2014.

Jaquith, Andrew. *Security Metrics: Replacing Fear, Uncertainty, and Doubt.* Addison Wesley Professional, 2007

Hubbard W, Douglas. *How to Measure Anything in Cybersecurity Risk*. Wiley, 2023

Shortridge, Kelly. *Security Chaos Engineering: Developing Resilience and Safety at Speed and Scale.* O'Reilly Media, 2023

Magnusson, Andres. *Practical Vulnerability Management: A Strategic Approach to Managing Cyber Risk.* No Starch Press, 2020.

Brikman, Yevgeniy. Terraform – Up and Running: Writing Infrastructure as Code. O'Reilly Media, 2022.

Dotson, Chris. *Practical Cloud Security: A Guide for Secure Design and Deployment.* O'Reilly, 2019.

RECOMMENDED TRAINING

• How to Career Guide into Cyber Security

https://www.udemy.com/course/how-to-career-guide-into-cyber-security/

• Software Supply Chain Security for Developers

https://www.udemy.com/course/software-supply-chain-security-for-developers/

OWASP TOP TEN WEB APP SECURITY RISKS

The OWASP Top Ten web application security risk document is a security reference for developers to aid with security. It is a consensus driven resource listing the most important security risks applicable to web application security. At the time of publication consists of:

- A01:2021 Broken Access Control
- A02:2021 Cryptographic Failures
- A03:2021 Injection
- A04:2021 Insecure Design
- A05:2021 Security Misconfiguration
- A06:2021 Vulnerable and Outdated Components
- A07:2021 Identification and Authentication Failures
- A08:2021 Software and Data Integrity Failures
- A09:2021 Security Logging and Monitoring Failures
- A10:2021 Server-Side Request Forgery (SSRF)

The online resource can be found at and it is highly recommended to follow this resource as first point of technical reference: https://owasp.org/www-project-top-ten/

OWASP TOP 10 API SECURITY RISKS

The OWASP Top Ten API security risk document is a security reference for developers to aid with security. It is a consensus driven resource listing the most important security risks applicable to API security. At the time of publication consists of:

- API1:2023 Broken Object Level Authorization
- API2:2023 Broken Authentication
- API3:2023 Broken Object Property Level Authorisation
- API4:2023 Unrestricted Resource Consumption
- API5:2023 Broken Function Level Authorization
- API6:2023 Unrestricted Access to Sensitive Business Flows
- API7:2023 Server-Side Request Forgery
- API8:2023 Security Misconfiguration
- API9:2023 Improper Inventory Management
- API10:2023 Unsafe Consumption of APIs

The online resource can be found at and it is highly recommended to follow this resource as first point of technical reference.

SECURITY BENCHMARKS

The Center for Internet Security, referred to as CIS, benchmarks are a collection of security documents that provide security configuration guidelines across multiple vendors. These can be used to securely configure the hardware and software assets that make up the development environment. Some applicable technology covered includes cloud providers, DevSecOps tools and operation systems.

The online resource for security configuration can be found following the link below and it is highly recommended to follow this resource as first point of technical reference:
https://www.cisecurity.org/cis-benchmarks

Also from CIS is the CIS critical security controls these are a prioritised and consensus driven best practices to implement security in the most efficient manner possible. At the time of publication consists of:

• Inventory and Control of Enterprise Assets

• Inventory and Control of Software Assets

• Data Protection

• Secure Configuration of Enterprise Assets & Software

• Account Management

• Access Control Management

- Continuous Vulnerability Management

- Audit Log Management

- Email and Web Browser Protections

- Malware Defences

- Data Recovery

- Network Infrastructure Management

- Network Monitoring and Defence

- Security Awareness and Skills Training

- Service Provider Management

- Application Software Security

- Incident Response Management

- Penetration Testing

The online resource for the critical security controls can be found: https://www.cisecurity.org/controls

RECOMMENDED ONLINE RESOURCES

- https://www.securityexceptions.com/blog/

- https://owasp.org/

- https://www.cisecurity.org/

- https://www.cybersecurity-insiders.com/

- https://www.darkreading.com/

- https://danielmiessler.com/

  https://owasp.org/www-project-proactive-controls/v3/en/c1-security-requirements

USEFUL SOFTWARE

• https://draw.io a no login registration design tool for creating designs for software solutions or security architecture purposes.

• https://cairis.org/ threat modelling, commercial solution.

• https://www.iriusrisk.com/ threat modelling, commercial solution.

• https://learn.microsoft.com/en-us/azure/security/develop/threat-modeling-tool threat modelling tool, free to use.

• https://owasp.org/www-project-threat-dragon/ threat modelling, free to use.

• https://threatmodeler.com/ threat modelling, commercial solution.

• https://about.gitlab.com/ developer security development platform.

• https://www.veracode.com/ application security development platform

CONTACTING THE AUTHOR

I can be contacted via LinkedIn, if you have the time, please do take the time to leave a review of this book. It helps to know what was useful and anything to add in future releases. If you have benefitted from the information and if you found it helpful do let me know.

https://www.linkedin.com/in/timcoakley/

Intentionally blank

ABOUT THE AUTHOR

Tim Coakley is a Senior Security Solutions Architect for a large multi-national organisation, an author and creator of numerous cyber security training resources from hands on labs through to specialist courses.

Tim started a long and successful full-time career in Digital Forensics supporting the criminal justice system and law enforcement on a long list of criminal cases. Parallel to this Tim operated a research and development business creating solutions from design through to sales and support resulting in some unique and niche software not developed anywhere else.

Tim now works fully within the cybersecurity space and has supported and worked within many security teams including, Investigations, Incident Response, Threat intelligence, Penetration Testing, Governance and Engineering until landing into Security Architecture.

Application Security is a profession in demand, specialist practitioners with skills in Application Security (AppSec) will increase significantly over the coming years. This book covers all of the essentials you need on the subject and does so in as concise manner as possible. This book is for cyber security professionals at all levels and stages in their career and was developed from years of experience working within the Cybersecurity industry.

Tim Coakley
Cybersecurity Professional and Author

Application Security Essentials, part of the Security Architecture series, you will learn about:

- What is Application Security
- What is Security Architecture
- Importance of Security Culture
- Secure Configuration
- Code Security
- API Security
- Identity Access Security
- Security Designs and Documentation

www.ingramcontent.com/pod-product-compliance
Lightning Source LLC
LaVergne TN
LVHW051703050326
832903LV00032B/3973